A great book for a great kid !!
You can read English, I hope,
because you sure can't speak it.

Anne Young.

Herbert Henning
16.10.91

REMNANTS OF GREEN

A Rainforest Journey

Anne Young and Herbert Heinrich

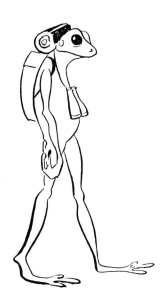

Kangaroo Press

© Wildlife Encounters 1989

First published in 1989 by Kangaroo Press Pty Ltd
3 Whitehall Road (P.O. Box 75) Kenthurst 2156
Typeset by G.T. Setters Pty Limited
Printed in Hong Kong by Colorcraft Ltd

ISBN 0 86417 271 0

Contents

The text for this book has been adapted from 'Remnants of Green... A Treatise on Six Rainforests', a research paper by Herbert Heinrich and Anne Young as part of their postgraduate studies in Plant and Wildlife Illustration, at Newcastle College of Advanced Education, during 1987.

The artwork is reproduced from the original watercolour paintings which are now part of the 'Remnants of Green' Rainforest Exhibit by Herbert Heinrich and Anne Young at Newcastle Regional Museum.

Introduction

This book is about various Australian rainforests of the <u>subtropical</u> region. These rainforests exist mainly along the coast of New South Wales and southern Queensland, and they are also found in relatively small pockets in the mountains of the Great Dividing Range.

They are remnants of much larger rainforests which, up until 60 million years ago, covered much of the Australian continent. These moist forests have slowly dwindled away over millions of years as our <u>climate</u> and <u>environment</u> have changed.

Our journey begins in the high mountain rainforests and will take us down the slopes and on to the <u>littoral</u> rainforests at sea level.

Note: The 'Glossary' in the back of this book gives more details about any of the words that are <u>underlined</u>.

On the Mountains

Rainforests of the high mountains are usually cold, dark and wet. They are often bathed in mists for days on end.

The trees are mostly the magnificent Antarctic beech. These forest giants often have a thick coat of mosses and lichens, and the bases are gnarled, twisted and massive. The largest beech trees are many hundreds of years old.

Small remaining pockets of Antarctic beech rainforest are the relics of the flora from millions of years ago when Gondwanaland was in a much cooler climate.

A beech rainforest is like a fairyland. It is so quiet that it becomes quite spooky. The only sound at times is the rain of constantly falling leaves forming a carpet on the forest floor. Bracket fungi and colonies of parasol fungi glisten like jewels in the eerie darkness.

Apart from a few <u>species</u> of ground ferns, the only other major lower level plants are the <u>tree-ferns</u>. These grow abundantly among the moss-covered rocks and rotting fallen timber. Here you will find the <u>beech orange fungus</u>. This unusual fungus grows only on Antarctic beech trees.

Snails often feed on <u>fungi</u>. The <u>snail</u> in the picture might eat the beech orange fungus, but it also eats worms and even other snails.

Occasionally thickets of fern and <u>tree-fern</u> provide good cover for the chicks of the <u>olive whistler</u>. These birds live only in this type of forest.

Food for the chicks is plentiful here. The bark of the beech tree is heavily flaked and provides homes for many small creatures.

The Antarctic beech is sometimes called the negrohead beech because of the shape of its crown.

Near the tops of the trees there is more sunlight and the branches are covered with other plants. Ferns, mosses, lichens, and orchids adorn every inch of the branches. The tree is a support for the plants, but they feed only on the moisture and nutrients on the outside of the tree without harming it. Plants like this are called epiphytes.

However as many branches and trunks are old and rotten, pieces of wood may break off with the extra weight of the epiphytes, and come crashing down.

In the Valleys

Let us go down in the deep gorges, cut by creeks that run almost continuously. Here the rainfall is still high and the soils are <u>fertile</u>, but the rainforests are different from those on the mountain tops.

Inside the rainforest it is dark because very little light can penetrate the interlocking <u>crowns</u> of the trees. The air is damp and cool, and is such a relief on a summer day.

There is no grass on the forest floor, just leaves of all shapes and sizes, large mosses and many ferns. Many birds are calling all around, and the sound of water babbling over the rocks in the river is ever present.

The music of the rainforest is only disturbed by the scratching sounds of the <u>spine-tailed logrunner</u>. It flings the leaf litter aside in its search for food.

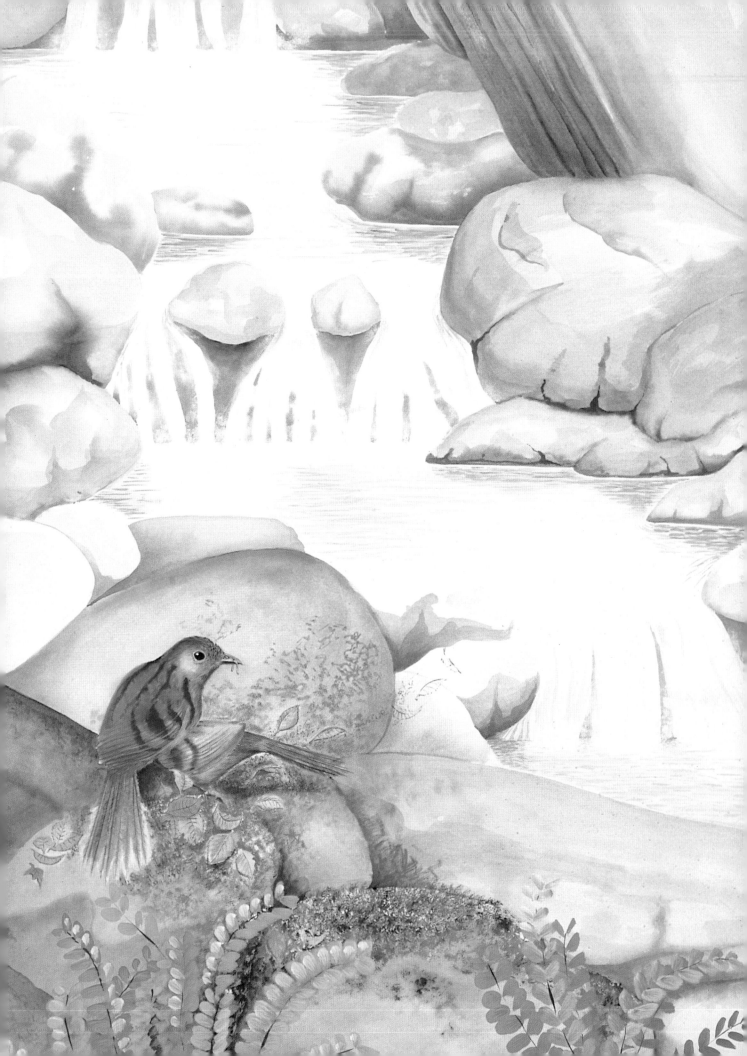

This type of rainforest has many species of trees. Most of them have very large, soft, shiny leaves. They need to catch any sunlight that might filter through the <u>canopy</u>.

The <u>tree-ferns</u> here are tall, with slender trunks. Sometimes they form a forest within a forest.

The female <u>wonder brown butterfly</u> moves along the trail in search of her food plant. She rests on low, sunlit leaves between her erratic fluttering. The males and the females look so different that until recently it was thought that they were two <u>species</u>.

Many of the trees have developed huge roots above the ground because there is not enough <u>oxygen</u> in the soil. A lot of this oxygen is used up by decaying <u>humus</u> on the ground.

The <u>yellow carrabeen tree</u> has huge <u>buttress roots</u> which provide large areas for oxygen. They also act as strong supports for the tall trunks reaching into the tangle of branches and leaves overhead.

<u>Bird-nest ferns</u> and <u>elkhorns</u> attach themselves to the trunks and these provide hiding places for many rainforest animals.

Birds are readily heard, but are difficult to see amongst the tangle of branches, <u>lianes</u> and leaves. High in the <u>canopy</u> the <u>yellow-tailed black cockatoo</u> visits the rainforest in its search for the wood-boring insects which make up a major part of its diet.

This huge bird maintains contact with the others of its group by constant wheezing and loud alarming squawks. Large shadows move from limb to limb as the flock seeks a place to rest. Their daily journey takes them to <u>habitats</u> beyond this rainforest.

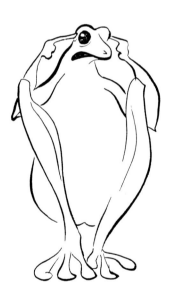

A more common resident of the rainforests in the valleys is the brush turkey. These birds have the peculiar habit of building mounds of decaying leaves in which they incubate their eggs.

The male tends the mound, continually piling up the leaves and unpiling them again, to maintain a constant temperature, till the young chicks hatch.

Rainforest fig trees are often known as <u>strangler figs</u>. The fig fruits are favoured by many birds. <u>Lewin's honeyeater</u> is one of the most common of rainforest birds. Its <u>staccato</u> calls ring loudly through the forest.

Birds may drop some of the seeds from fig fruits in the crevices of other trees. Here they <u>germinate</u> and grow. <u>Aerial roots</u> are sent down, and on reaching the ground they thicken and eventually grow together to completely envelop the host tree. The host tree is then strangled and rots away, leaving a hollow inside the strangler fig tree.

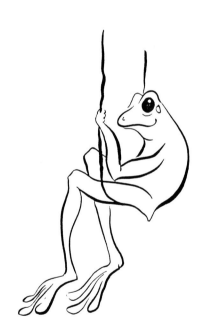

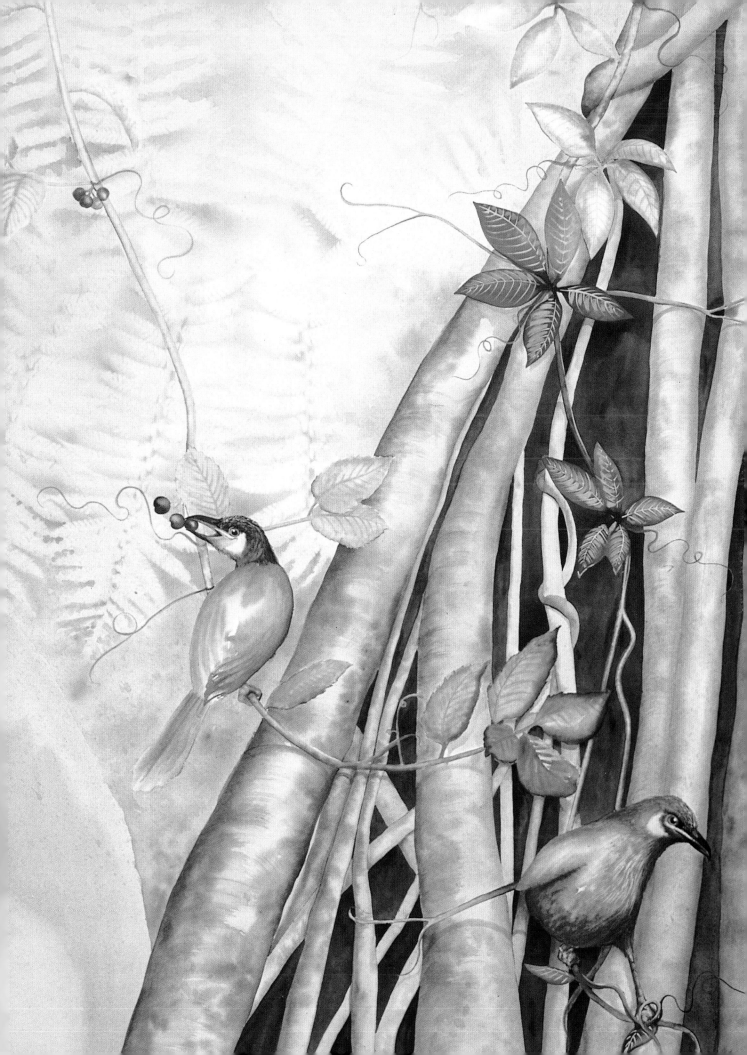

The tangle of vines provides perches for the inquisitive <u>rufous</u> <u>fantail</u> which seems to ambush any visitor to its home. Sometimes it flutters within an arm's length. This may be a welcome or possibly a warning... for in the <u>canopy</u> grows the dreaded <u>stinging</u> <u>tree</u>. The large heart-shaped leaves are translucent in the sunlight and are covered with tiny hairs which will cause a very nasty sting if touched.

Most rainforest flowers are difficult to see because they grow up above the <u>canopy</u> of intermingling branches and leaves. Wherever there is sunlight there are flowers, and wherever there are flowers there are usually butterflies.

The <u>common Jezabel butterfly</u> flutters over the treetops in search of the <u>nectar</u> of the blossoms. A common source of food for this insect is this <u>mistletoe</u>.

Mistletoes are <u>parasitic plants</u> that grow from a sticky seed dropped onto the branches of host trees.

Further down the mountains, where it is warmer and the soils are deeper, another type of valley rainforest grows. Here there is less rainfall and little gullies support the flora and fauna.

Some eucalypt trees like the flooded gum compete for space in these forests. Gum tree seedlings find it very difficult to survive in the darkness of the rainforest. When a large tree falls, however, there may be enough sunlight for some of them to grow.

The greenhood orchid also likes sunny patches and stands proudly among the variety of ferns and fungi.

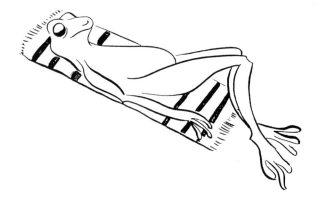

This rainforest has many <u>bangalow palms</u>. Their tree trunks are slender and tall, and most of them support <u>climbing fishbone ferns</u>.

Some special rainforest birds like the <u>green catbird</u> may live here. Its call is very distinctive and true to its name, but its colouring is such an effective <u>camouflage</u> that it is rarely seen. You will not see it in this picture.

During the summer evenings, flocks of grey-headed fruit bats come to feed on the fruits of the forest trees.

These mammals are very noisy and are often heard fighting and squabbling in the treetops.

At first glance the rainforest is nothing but green leaves, but amongst the light and dark patches many colourful flowers and fruits can be seen.

Bangalow palms produce masses of red berries which hang like necklaces. The forest floor is scattered with the fruits that have been dropped by the feeding mammals and birds.

Many of the rainforest trees in the valleys have been used to make furniture.

Trees like the softwood red cedar were cut and floated down the rivers to sawmills and waiting ships. Sadly, today there are few cedar trees left.

The pioneering settlers followed the cedar-getters and cleared much of the rainforests for farming. Eucalypts began to grow because the shady canopy was broken.

By the Sea

Littoral or coastal rainforests are usually very different from the other types of rainforest we have passed through. They may occur on outcrops of volcanic rock like headlands and offshore islands, or in sheltered sand dunes behind beaches.

The trees in these rainforests do not grow very tall because the soil is usually shallow and they are exposed to the salty sea air. It is difficult to get into the forest itself because of the tangle of vines.

Eastern yellow robins seem to play 'hide-and-seek' behind the hanging lianes. When the bell-like piping changes to longer whistles it means that they are looking for a mate.

Many rainforest birds are coloured yellow. They are well-hidden in the dappled light of the forest. The <u>regent bowerbird</u> may be invisible if it sits still.

One of the most common trees in <u>littoral</u> rainforests is <u>Fraser's sandpaper fig tree</u>. Aborigines used the leaves of this tree to smooth their spears and to sharpen their tools.

During the day, colonies of fruit-bats roost in the spreading crown of the strangler fig tree. Here they are protected from the sun, and at night they will feed on the delicious fig fruits.

This tree has also become host to many ferns, orchids, mistletoes and lianes. So little light gets through to the ground that few plants grow here. The rainforest floor is clear except for a carpet of leaves.

These warmer areas are good <u>habitats</u> for reptiles. This <u>skink</u> is commonly seen basking in the patches of sunlight. It needs warmth to become active enough to hunt for food.

Like many lizards it will throw off its tail if attacked. Luckily it will soon grow another.

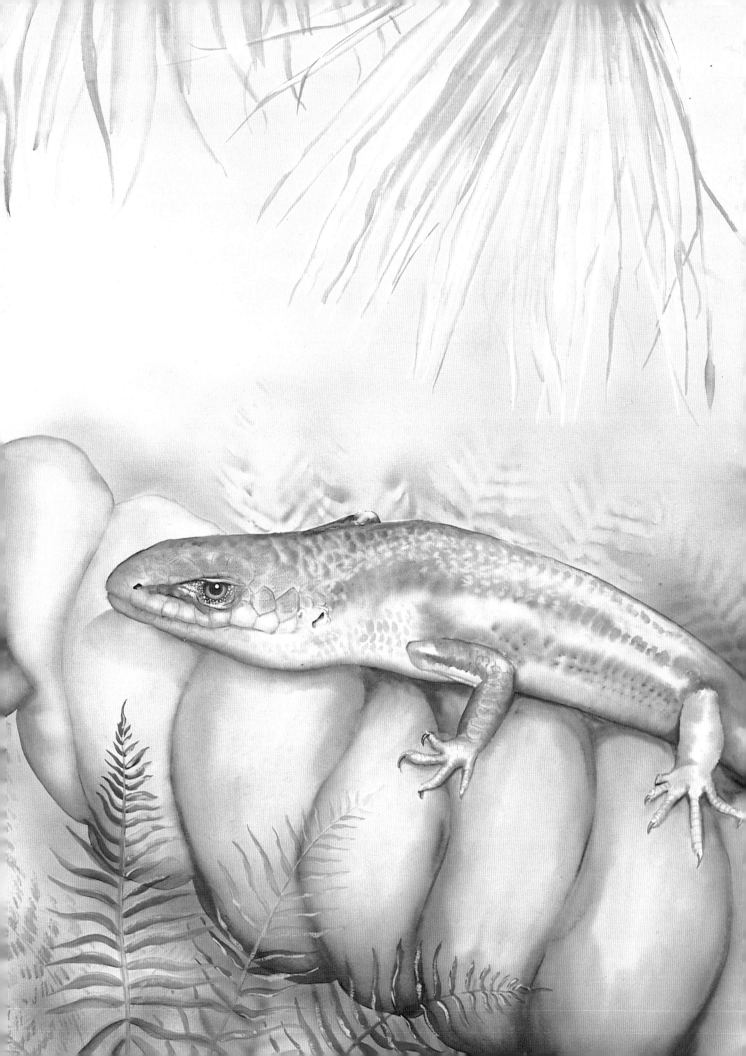

Peron's tree frog feeds here at night on the forest floor. His loud call rattles through the rainforest and mingles with the slow whine of the sea breeze in the treetops.

This frog has a clever camouflage. It can change the colour of its skin. When the light is bright, the emerald green spots help hide it among the rainforest leaves.

The agile <u>ringtail possum</u> climbs among the fronds of the <u>cabbage-tree palm</u>. It does not seem to notice the razor-sharp barbs along the shaft of the fan-leaf.

These <u>marsupials</u> often build a nest of rolled-up fern fronds in the fork of a small tree. The nest is called a drey.

At night, possums can be observed by torchlight. During the warmer months, the female may be seen with one or two young riding on her back.

Many of the tiny birds like <u>silvereyes</u> move around the forest in small parties for protection from larger <u>predators</u>. They perform gymnastic feats while feeding on the fruits of the <u>koda tree</u>.

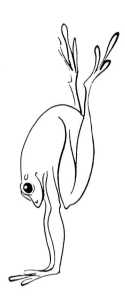

These birds also enjoy eating fruits in planted orchards and so are often thought of as pests. They can ruin large fruits by pecking holes in the skin. But here in the rainforest, there is plenty of food for all the residents.

This rainforest journey has taken us from the tops of the mountains down the slopes, and on to the seashore.

We have looked at some habitats, and some of the animals and plants that live there. The <u>crimson rosellas</u> are among the lucky ones because they are at home in most rainforests. The rainforest remnants that we still have are very important to those animals and plants that have nowhere else to live.

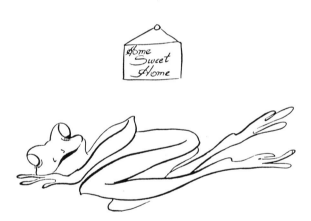

The remnants of green discussed in this book can be found in isolated pockets in this area of Australia.

Australia's rainforests would fit into a circle of 80 kilometres radius. They are scattered over 0.3 per cent of Australia's land area. This is about one quarter of the rainforests existing 200 years ago when Europeans first arrived.

On a world scale rainforests are disappearing at a rate of the size of a football field every second. More than 40 per cent of the world's rainforest has already been cleared by man.

The Australian rainforest remnants and many of the inhabitants are in danger of being lost within our own lifetimes.

Glossary

(in alphabetical order)

aerial roots roots hanging down to the ground from plants that are growing on another tree

altitude height above sea level

Antarctic beech tree *Nothofagus moorei*

bangalow palm *Archontophoenix cunninghamiana*

beech orange fungus a species of the genus *Cyttaria*

bird-nest fern *Asplenium flaccidum* and *Asplenium australasicum*

brush turkey *Alectura lathami*

buttress roots raised spreading roots, like wall supports, at the base of a tree

cabbage-tree palm *Livistona australis*

camouflage colour and shape that blend into the background

canopy leaves and branches at the tops of trees overlapping to form a complete cover

climate the pattern of weather conditions that affect plant and animal growth

climbing fishbone fern *Arthropteris tenella*

common Jezabel butterfly *Delias nigrina*

colonies large groups of the same plants or same animals living together

crimson rosella *Platycercus elegans*

crown the top part of a tree which contains the branches and leaves

eastern yellow robin *Eopsaltria australis*

environment all the conditions in which a plant or animal lives e.g. temperature, light, water, other plants and animals

elkhorn *Platycerium bifurcatum*

epiphyte a plant that is attached to another plant, but does not feed on it

eucalypts a term for Australian gum trees of which there are over 500 species

fauna the animal population of a place; includes birds, insects and reptiles etc.

fertile soil capable of providing nourishment for plants to grow

flooded gum tree *Eucalyptus grandis*

flora the plant population of a place; includes non-flowering plants and fungi

Fraser's sandpaper fig tree *Ficus fraseri*

fungi a group of plants including mushrooms; they help to decompose plant and animal residues

germinates a seed sprouts a shoot and a root

Gondwanaland the ancient large landmass when the World's southern continents were joined

green catbird *Ailuroedus crassirostris*

greenhood orchid *Pterostylis grandiflora*

grey-headed fruit bat *Pteropus poliocephalus*

habitat   a place or environment in which any given plant or animal lives

humus   organic matter resulting from the decay of plant and animal tissue

incubate   to maintain correct temperature for the development of chicks in eggs

koda tree   *Ehretia acuminata*

Lewin's honeyeater   *Meliphaga lewinii*

lianes   climbing plants with long woody rope-like stems

littoral   close to the seashore

mammals   animals that suckle their young with milk; all mammals grow hair

marsupials   a class of mammals; the young are born early, then develop in the mother's pouch

mistletoe   *Amylotheca dictyophleba*

nectar   a sugary fluid in the base of a flower, attractive to insects, birds and small mammals

nutrients   elements of food that are of value to living things

olive whistler   *Pachycephala olivacea*

oxygen in soil   air is usually in soil, but may be displaced by excess water as in rainforests

parasitic plants   live on a host plant from which they obtain their food; they may be harmful if too many are on the same host

Peron's tree frog   *Litoria peronii*

predator   an animal that eats other animals

red cedar tree   *Toona australis*

regent bowerbird   *Sericulus chrysocephalus*

ringtail possum   *Pseudocheirus peregrinus*

rufous fantail   *Rhipidura rufifrons*

silvereye   *Zosterops lateralis*

skink   *Carlia tetradactyla*

snail   a species of the genus *Strangesta*

species   a group of individuals able to breed among themselves, but not with another species

spine-tailed logrunner   *Orthonyx temminckii*

staccato   sounds that are abrupt and sharply cut off

stinging tree   *Dendrocnide excelsa*

strangler fig tree   various species including the deciduous fig *Ficus superba*

subtropical   in the region just to the south of the Tropic of Capricorn; here we mean southern Queensland and New South Wales

tree-ferns   at high altitude: *Dicksonia antarctica*;
   at lower altitude: various *Cyathea* species

yellow carrabeen tree   *Sloanea woollsii*

yellow-tailed black cockatoo   *Calyptorhynchus funereus*

wonder brown butterfly   *Heteronympha mirifica*